50
MORE CROCHETED
AFGHAN BORDERS

by Jean Leinhauser

Produced by

Production Team

Creative Directors: Jean Leinhauser and Rita Weiss

Senior Technical Editor: Ellen W. Liberles

Editors: Mary Ann Frits and Susan Lowman

Photographer: Carol Wilson Mansfield

Pattern Testers: Carrie Cristiano and Mary Ann Frits

Book Design: Linda Causee

Published by Leisure Arts

© 2009 by Leisure Arts, Inc.,
5701 Ranch Drive
Little Rock, AR 72223
www.leisurearts.com

All rights reserved. This publication is protected under federal copyright laws. Reproduction or distribution of this publication or any other Leisure Arts publication, including publications which are out of print, is prohibited unless specifically authorized. This includes, but is not limited to, any form of reproduction or distribution on or through the Internet, including posting, scanning, or e-mail transmission.

Although we have made every effort to be sure that these instructions are accurate and complete, we are not responsible for any typographical errors, or mistakes, or for variations in the work of individuals.

INTRODUCTION

Like the frosting on the cupcake, or the tiara on the bride, a beautiful border is the finishing touch for a lovingly created knitted or crocheted afghan.

Borders can be elegant or whimsical, can match or contrast with the afghan, and can lift even the simplest afghan from "ordinary" into the "very special" category.

If you usually depend upon fringe as an accent, you'll have fun experimenting with the 50 borders in this book

You won't find any gauge specified in our instructions, or any specific yarns or amounts mentioned. That's because you can choose to work the borders in any yarn that works well with the body of the afghan. You can use baby, sport or worsted weight, but avoid heavy, textured or fuzzy yarns because they don't work well for borders. If the afghan body is made with one of those yarns, choose a smooth yarn, perhaps in a contrasting color, for the border.

We've shown some borders worked in more than one color, but you can make them in one color if you prefer. And some of the borders we show in one color you can easily work in two or more colors for a completely different look.

Have fun with these borders. You're sure to find just the perfect one for your masterpiece.

Jean Leinhauser

HOW TO USE THE BORDERS

PREPARING THE CROCHETED AFGHAN

When the afghan body is completed, use the main color or another complimentary color to work a single crochet edging around all four sides. Although our borders are designed to be worked on each end, not on the sides, working this edging on the sides will even out the rows and give a more finished look.

To work the edging. hold the afghan with the right side facing you, and join the yarn with a sl st in the top right corner.

Edging Round

Ch 1, work 3 sc in same st as joining; work sc evenly across top, bottom and sides, working 3 sc in each of the remaining 3 outer corners, and adjusting sts as needed to keep work flat. Finish off and weave in all yarn ends securely.

PREPARING THE KNITTED AFGHAN

When the afghan body is completed, use the main color or another complimentary color to work a single crochet edging on the top (usually the bound-off edge) and the bottom (usually the cast-on edge) of the afghan. Because crochet stitches are bulkier than knit stitches, you may need to adjust your sc stitches to keep the work flat. Do this by skipping a knit stitch here and there as needed.

Top Edging Row

To work the edging, hold the afghan with the right side facing you, and the bound-off edge at the top. Using a crochet hook, join the yarn with a sl st in the top right corner, ch 1, sc in the same st.

Sc in each bound-off stitch across, skipping sts as needed to keep work flat. Finish off, weave in all yarn ends securely

Bottom Edging Row.

Hold afghan with right side facing you and the cast-on edge at the top. Using a crochet hook, join the yarn with a sl st in the top right corner, ch 1, sc in the same st.

Sc in each cast-on stitch across, skipping sts as needed to keep work flat. Finish off, weave in all yarn ends securely.

MULTIPLES

Each border pattern starts with a "multiple" that looks like this:

Stitch Multiple: 6 + 2 sts

A multiple is the number of stitches needed to complete one unit of a pattern. In this book, a multiple means the number of stitches required in the foundation row to work the first row of a border and have it come out even. In the example of a 6 + 2 multiple, you will need to have any number of stitches which is divisible evenly by 6: 72 or 144 or 288. To this number you will add the + 2.

The correct multiple should be established when you work the Foundation Row given with each border pattern. You can skip or add stitches in that row to achieve the multiple. Multiples are counted from corner to corner on the end on which the border will be worked.

When counting stitches on the afghan to determine the border, it is helpful to place a small safety pin in every 10th or 20th stitch.

ESTIMATING YARN AMOUNTS

Measure the edge of the afghan to which the border will be attached, and multiply by two. If the afghan is 40" wide, the top and bottom borders will count as 80".

Next with scrap yarn of the same weight you plan to use for the border, make a chain about 12" long in the stitch multiple given in the border pattern you've chosen, plus one more chain. Work all the rows of the border starting on chain. Then rip out the work and measure the yarn you used in the 12" sample. This will give you the approximate yardage needed for each 12" of border. To this add at least 10 % extra for added insurance.

ABBREVIATIONS AND SYMBOLS

Crochet patterns are written in a special shorthand which is used so that instructions don't take up too much space. They sometimes seem confusing, but once you learn them, you'll have no trouble following them.

These are Abbreviations

Beg	beginning
Cl(s)	cluster(s)
Ch(s)	chain(s)
Dc	double crochet
DcCl	double crochet cluster
Dtr	double triple crochet
Hdc	half double crochet
Inc	Increase(ing)
Lp(s)	loop(s)
Patt	pattern
PC	popcorn
Prev	previous
Rem	remaining
Rep	repeat(ing)
Rnd(s)	round(s)
Sc	single crochet
Sl st	slip stitch
Sp(s)	space(s)
St(s)	stitch(es)
Tog	together
Tr	triple crochet
TrCl	triple cluster
TrPC	triple crochet popcorn
V-st	V-stitch
YO	yarn over hook

These are standard Symbols

*An asterisk (or double asterisks**) in a pattern row, indicates a portion of instructions to be used more than once. For instance, "rep from * three times" means that after working the instructions once, you must work them again three times for a total of 4 times in all.

†A dagger (or double daggers ††) indicates that those instructions will be repeated again later in the same row or round.

:The number of stitches after a colon tells you the number of stitches you will have when you have completed the row or round.

( ) Parentheses are used in two ways. First, they enclose copy to be worked the number of times indicated following the parentheses. For instance "(dc in next 3 dc, ch 1) 3 times" means that you are to work the instructions within the parentheses a total of 3 times.

Parentheses are also use to set off or clarify a group of stitches to be worked into the same space or stitch. For instance, "(dc, ch 2, dc) in corner sp".

[ ] Brackets and ( ) parentheses are also used to give you additional information.

These are standard Terms

Front Loop—This is the loop toward you at the top of the crochet stitch.

Back Loop—This is the loop away from you at the top of the crochet stitch.

Post—This is the vertical part of the crochet stitch.

Join—This means to join with a sl st unless another stitch is specified.

Finish Off—This means to cut the yarn, leaving a 6" yarn end to weave in later. Then pull the cut yarn end through the last loop on the hook. This keeps the work from unraveling.

The patterns in this book have been written using the crochet terminology that is used in the United States. Terms which may have different equivalents in other parts of the world are listed below.

United States	International
Double crochet (dc)	treble crochet (tr)
Gauge	tension
Half double crochet (hdc)	half treble crochet (htr)
Single crochet (sc)	double crochet
Skip	miss
Slip stitch	single crochet
Triple crochet (tr)	double treble crochet (dtr)
Yarn over (YO)	yarn forward (yfwd)
Yarn over (YO)	Yarn over hook (YOH)

CROCHET HOOKS

US	B-1	C-2	D-3	E-4	F-5	G-6	7	H-8	I-9	J-10	K-10½	L-11	M/N-13	N/P-15	P/Q	Q	S
Metric	2.25	2.75	3.25	3.5	3.75	4	4.5	5	5.5	6	6.5	8	9	10	15	16	19

#1

Stitch multiple: 10 + 7 sts

Yarn: One color

Stitch Guide

V-Stitch (V-st): In specified st work (tr, ch 4, tr): V-st made.

Shell: In specified sp work (2 tr, ch 4, 2 tr): shell made.

Fan: In specified sp work (tr, ch 1) 6 times, tr in same sp: fan made.

Instructions

Foundation Row (wrong side): With wrong side facing you, join yarn with sc in first st at right; sc in each rem st; ch 4 (counts as a tr on following row), turn.

Row 1 (right side): Skip next 2 sc, V-st in next sc; *skip 4 sc, V-st in next sc; rep from * across to last 3 sc, skip 2 sc, tr in last sc; ch 4, turn.

Row 2: Work shell in ch-4 sp of next V-st, ch 1; *work 3 tr in ch-4 sp of next V-st, ch 1, work shell in ch-4 sp of next V-st ch 1; rep from * across, ending last rep with tr in top of turning ch-4; ch 4, turn.

Row 3: Work fan in ch-4 sp of next shell; *skip next 2 tr of same shell, sc in next tr, ch 4, skip next tr, sc in next tr; work fan in ch-4 sp of next shell; rep from * across, tr in top of turning ch-4. Finish off; weave in yarn ends.

#2

Stitch multiple: 6 + 3 sts

Yarn: One color

Stitch Guide

Triple Crochet Popcorn (trPC): Work 5 tr in specified st; drop lp from hook, insert hook from front to back in top of first dc made, pick up dropped lp and draw though lp on hook: trPC made.

Instructions

Foundation Row (wrong side): With wrong side facing you, join yarn with sc in first st at right; sc in each st, ch 4 (counts as a dc and ch-1 sp on following row), turn.

Row 1: Skip first 2 sc, dc in next sc; *ch 1, skip next sc, dc in next sc; rep from * across; ch 1, turn.

Row 2: Sc in each dc and in each ch-1 sp across, ending last rep with sc in turning ch sp, sc in 3rd ch of turning ch-4; ch 4, turn.

Row 3: Skip first 2 sc; *trPC in next sc, ch 4,** skip next 2 sc, sc in next sc, ch 4, skip next 2 sc; rep from * across, ending last rep at **; skip 2 sc, sc in last sc. Finish off; weave in yarn ends.

#3

Stitch multiple: 4 + 1 sts

Yarn: Two colors, Color A and Color B

Instructions

Foundation Row: With wrong side facing you, join Color A with sc in first st at right; sc in each rem st; ch 6 (counts as a dc and ch-3 sp on following row), turn.

Row 1 (right side): Skip 3 sc, dc in next sc; *ch 3, skip 3 sc, dc in next sc; rep from * across; ch 1, turn.

Row 2: Sc in first sc; *ch 3, skip next ch-3 sp, sc in next dc; rep from * across, ending last rep with ch 3, sc in 3rd ch of turning ch-6; ch 1, turn.

Row 3: Sc in first sc; *in next ch-3 sp work (sc, ch 2, 4 dc, hdc, sc); rep from * across, ending sc in last sc; do not ch, turn.

Row 4: Sl st in first sc, ch 3, working behind sts on Row 2, sc in next ch-3 sp of Row 1; *ch 4, sc in next ch-3 sp of Row 2; rep from * across, ending sc in side of last sc on Row 2. Finish off Color A.

Row 5 (right side): With right side facing you, join Color B with sc in first sc; *in next ch-4 sp work (sc, ch 3, 4 tr, dc, hdc, sc); rep from * across to ch-3 sp, skip ch-3 sp, sc in last sl st. Finish off; weave in yarn ends.

#4

Stitch multiple: 7 + 1 sts

Yarn: One color

Instructions

Foundation Row (wrong side): With wrong side facing you, join yarn with sc in first st at right; sc in each rem st; ch 4 (counts as a tr on following row), turn.

Row 1 (right side): Skip next sc, *tr in each of next 2 sc, ch 3, tr in each of next 2 sc,** skip next 3 sc; rep from * across, ending last rep at **; skip next sc, tr in last sc; ch 1, turn.

Row 2: Skip first tr, sc between first tr and next 2-tr pair, ch 5; *work (sc, ch 3, sc) in next ch-3 sp, ch 5 **, sc between next two 2-tr pairs, ch 5; rep from * across, ending last rep at **; sc between last pair of 2-tr and turning ch. Finish off; weave in yarn ends.

#5

Stitch multiple: 6 + 1 sts

Yarn: One color

Stitch Guide

V-Stitch (V-st): In specified st work (dc, ch 2, dc): V-st made.

Shell: In specified st work (3 dc, ch 3, 3 dc): shell made.

Instructions

Foundation Row (wrong side): With wrong side facing you, join yarn with sc in first st at right; sc in each rem st, ch 5 (counts as dc and ch-2 sp on following row), turn.

Row 1: *Skip next 2 sc, work V-st in next sc, ch 2, skip next 2 sc, dc in next sc**; ch 2; rep from * across, ending last rep at **; ch 4 (counts as dc and ch-1 sp on following row), turn.

Row 2: *Shell in ch-2 sp of next V-st, ch 1**; dc in next dc, ch 1; rep from * across, ending last rep at **; dc in 3rd ch of turning ch-5; ch 1, turn.

Row 3: Sc in first dc; *work 7 dc in ch-3 sp of next shell, sc in next dc; rep from * across, ending last rep with sc in 3rd ch of turning ch-4. Finish off; weave in yarn ends.

#6

Stitch multiple: 3 + 1 sts

Yarn: Two colors, Color A and Color B

Instructions

Note: *All rows are worked on the right side.*

Foundation Row (right side): With right side facing you, join Color A with sc in first st at right; sc in each rem st. Finish off Color A.

Row 1 (right side): With right side facing you, join Color B with sc in top of first sc at right; sc in next 2 sc; *ch 1, skip next sc, sc in next 2 sc; rep from * across, ending last rep with sc in last 3 (instead of 2) sc. Finish off Color B.

Row 3 (right side): With right side facing you, join Color A with sl st in first sc at right, ch 2; *skip next 2 sc; in next ch-1 sp work 3 hdc, ch 3, sl st in hdc at base of ch-3 just made; rep from * across to last 3 sc, skip 2 sc, hdc in last sc. Finish off; weave in yarn ends.

#7

Stitch multiple: 3 + 2 sts

Yarn: Two colors, Color A and Color B

Stitch Guide

Popcorn (PC): Work 5 dc in specified st; drop lp from hook, insert hook from front to back in top of first dc of group, hook dropped lp and draw through lp on hook: PC made.

Instructions

Foundation Row (wrong side): With wrong side facing you, join Color A with sc in first st at right; sc in next st and each rem st; ch 1, turn.

Row 1 (right side): Sc in each sc across; at end of row, finish off Color A.

Row 2 (right side): With right side facing you, join Color B in first sc at right, ch 2 (counts as a hdc), hdc in next sc; *PC in next sc, ch 1, hdc in next 2 sc; rep from * across; ch 1, turn.

Row 3: Sc in first 2 hdc, sc in next ch-1 sp, skip next PC; *sc in next 2 hdc, sc in next ch-1 sp, skip next PC; rep from * across, ending last rep with sc in last 2 hdc; ch 4 (counts as first tr of following rnd), turn.

Row 4: Work 2 tr in base of ch; *4 dc in next sc, 3 dc in next sc; rep from * across, ending last rep with 3 tr in last st. Finish off Color B.

Row 5 (right side): With right side facing, join Color A with a sc in 4th ch of ch-4 at right; *ch 3, skip next st, sc in next st; rep from * across. Finish off; weave in all yarn ends.

#8

Stitch multiple: 10 + 2 sts

Yarn: One color

Instructions

Foundation Row (right side): With right side facing you, join yarn with sc in first st at right; sc in each rem st; ch 1, turn.

Row 1: Sc in first sc, ch 3, sc in next sc; *ch 9, skip next 8 sc, sc in next sc, ch 3, sc in next sc; rep from * across; ch 1, turn.

Row 2: In first ch-3 sp work (sc, ch 4, sc); *in next ch-9 lp work (5 dc, sc, ch 4, sc, 5 dc); in next ch-3 sp work (sc, ch 4, sc); rep from * across. Finish off; weave in yarn ends.

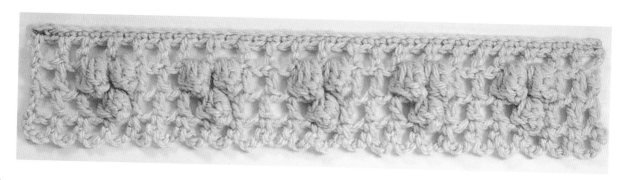

#9

Stitch multiple: 8 + 5 sts

Yarn: One color

Stitch Guide

Popcorn (PC): Work 4 dc in specified sp; drop lp from hook, insert hook from front to back in top of first dc of group, pick up dropped lp and draw through lp on hook: PC made.

Instructions

Foundation Row (right side): With right side facing you, join yarn with sc in first st at right; sc in each rem st; ch 4 (counts as a dc and ch-1 sp on following row), turn.

Row 1: Skip next sc, dc in next sc; *ch 1, skip next sc, dc in next sc; rep from * across, ending last rep with dc in last sc; ch 4, turn.

Row 2 (right side): Skip next ch-1 sp, dc in next dc, ch 1, dc in next dc; *work PC in next ch-1 sp, ch 2, skip next dc, PC in next ch-1 sp, dc in next dc; (ch 1, dc in next dc) twice; rep from * across, ending last rep with dc in 3rd ch of turning ch-4; finish off.

Row 3 (right side): With right side facing, join yarn with sl st in 3rd ch of turning ch-4; ch 4 (counts as a dc and ch-1 sp), skip next ch-1 sp, (dc in next dc, ch 1) twice; *skip next PC, work PC in ch-2 sp, skip next PC, dc in next dc; (ch 1, dc in next dc) twice; rep from * across, ending last rep with dc in 3rd ch of turning ch-4 ; ch 1, turn.

Row 4: Sc in first dc; (ch 4, sc in next dc) twice, ch 4; *sc in top of next PC, (ch 4, sc in next dc) 3 times, **ch 4; rep from * across, ending last rep at **. Finish off; weave in yarn ends.

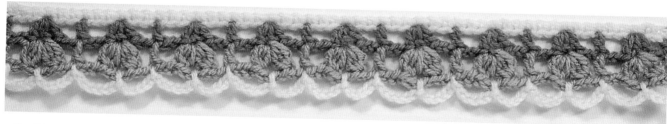

#10

Stitch multiple: 6 + 1 sts

Yarn: Three colors, Color A, Color B and Color C

Stitch Guide

Shell: Work 3 dc in specified st: shell made.

Double crochet cluster (dcCl): *YO, insert hook in specified st and draw up a lp, YO and draw through 2 lps on hook; rep from * twice in same st, YO and draw through 4 lps on hook: dcCl made.

Instructions

Note: *All rows are worked on right side.*

Foundation Row (right side): With right side facing you, join Color A with sc in first st at right; sc in each rem st; finish off Color A.

Row 1 (right side): With right side facing you, join Color B with sl st in first sc at right, ch 5 (counts as a dc and ch-2 sp), skip 2 sc; *shell in next sc, ch 2, skip 2 sc, dc in next sc, **ch 2, skip 2 sc; rep from * across, ending last rep at **; finish off Color B.

Row 2 (right side): With right side facing you, join Color C with sl st in 3rd ch of ch-5 at right, ch 5 (counts as a dc and ch-2 sp); *in center dc of next shell work (dcCl, ch 2, dcCl), ch 2, dc in next dc, ch 2; rep from * across, ending last rep with dc in top of last dc; finish off Color C.

Row 3 (right side): With right side facing you, join Color A with sc in 3rd ch of ch-5 at right; *ch 6, sl st in ch-2 sp between next 2 dcCls, ch 6, sl st in next dc; rep from * across, ending last rep with sc in last dc. Finish off Color A; weave in yarn ends.

12

#11

Stitch multiple: 10 + 1

Yarn: One Color

Instructions

Foundation Row (wrong side): With wrong side facing you, join yarn with sc in first st at right, sc in each rem st; ch 3 (counts as dc on following row), turn.

Row 1 (right side): Dc in next sc and in each sc across; ch 6 (counts as dc and ch-3 sp on following row), turn.

Row 2: Skip next 2 dc, sc in next 5 dc; *ch 7, skip next 5 dc, sc in next 5 dc; rep from * across to last 3 sts; ch 3, skip next 2 dc, dc in 3rd ch of turning ch-3; ch 5 (counts as tr and ch-1 sp on following row), turn.

Row 3: Dc in base of ch; ch 1, dc in next ch-3 sp, ch 1; *dc in next sc; (skip next sc, dc in next sc) 2 times, ch 1**; in next ch-7 lp work (dc, ch 1, dc, ch 3, dc, ch 1, dc), ch 1; rep from * across, ending last rep at **; dc in turn-ing ch-6 lp, ch 1, (dc, ch 1, tr) in 3rd ch of turning ch-6; ch 1, turn.

Row 4: Work 2 sc in first tr, sc in next ch-1 sp, sc in next dc, sc in next ch-1 sp; *ch 5, skip next dc and ch-1 sp, skip next 3 dc, skip next ch-1 sp and dc; sc in next ch-1 sp and in next dc; **work 5 sc in next ch-3 sp, sc in next dc and in next ch-1 sp; rep from * across, ending last rep at **; sc in turning ch-5 sp, 2 sc in 4th ch of turning ch-5; ch 7 (counts as tr and ch-3 sp on following row), turn.

Row 5: *Work 5 tr in next ch-5 sp, ch 3, **skip next 4 sc; dc in next sc, ch 3; rep from * across, ending last rep at **; tr in last sc; ch 1, turn.

Row 6: Sc in first tr; *3 sc in next ch-3 sp, ch 7**; 3 sc in next ch-3 sp, sc in next dc; rep from * across, ending last rep at **; 3 sc in turning ch-7 lp, sc in 4th ch of turning ch-7; ch 1, turn.

Row 7: Sc in first sc; *in next ch-7 lp work (tr, ch 3) 6 times, tr in same ch-7 lp**; skip next 3 sc, sc in next sc, skip next 3 sc; rep from * across, ending last rep at **; skip next 3 sc, sc in last sc. Finish off; weave in yarn ends.

#12

Stitch multiple: 6 + 2 sts

Yarn: One color

Stitch Guide:

Shell: In specified sp work (sc, hdc, dc, tr, ch 4, tr, dc, hdc, sc): shell made.

Instructions

Foundation Row (right side): With right side facing you, join yarn with sc in first st at right; sc in each st, ch 3 (counts as a dc on following row), turn.

Row 1: Dc in each of next 2 sc; *ch 2, skip 2 sc, dc in next sc; rep from * across, ending last rep with dc in each of last 3 sc; ch 1, turn.

Row 2 (right side): Sc in first dc; *work shell in next ch-2 sp, ** in next ch-2 sp work (sl st, ch 3, sl st); rep from * across, ending last rep at **; skip 2 dc, sc in top of turning ch-3. Finish off; weave in yarn ends.

13

#13

Stitch multiple: 4 + 1 sts

Yarn: One color

Instructions

Foundation Row: With right side facing you, join yarn with sc in first st at right, sc in each rem st, ch 1, turn.

Row 1: Sc in first 2 sc; *ch-5, skip next sc, sc in next 3 sc; rep from * to last 3 sc, ch 5, skip next sc, sc in last 2 sc; ch 1, turn.

Row 2: Sc in first sc; *ch 3, skip next sc, sc in next ch-5 sp, ch 3, skip next sc, sc in next sc; rep from * across; ch 1, turn.

Row 3: Sc in first sc and in next ch-3 sp; *ch 5, skip next sc, sc in next ch-3 sp, sc in next sc, sc in next ch-3 sp; rep from * across, ending ch 5, skip next sc, sc in next ch-3 sp, sc in last sc; ch 1, turn.

Row 4: Sc in first sc; *ch 7, skip next sc, skip next ch-5 sp and skip next sc; in next sc work (sc, ch 5, sc); rep from * across, ending ch 7, skip next sc, skip next ch-5 sp and next sc, sc in last sc. Finish off; weave in yarn ends.

#14

Stitch multiple: 6 + 1

Yarn: Two colors, Color A and Color B

Stitch Guide

Shell: In specified st or sp work (2 dc, ch 1) twice, 2 dc in same st or sp: shell made.

V-stitch (V-st): In specified st work (dc, ch 1, dc): V-stitch made.

Instructions

Foundation Row (wrong side): With wrong side facing you, join Color A with sc in first st at right; sc in next st and each rem st; ch 1, turn.

Row 1: Sc in each sc across; at end of row, do not ch or turn; finish off Color A.

Row 2 (right side): With right side facing you, join Color B with sl st in first sc at right; ch 3 (counts as a dc), in same sc work (dc, ch 1, 2 dc), skip next 2 sc; *sc in next sc, skip 2 sc, shell in next sc, skip 2 sc; rep from * across to last 4 sc, sc in next sc, skip 2 sc, in last sc work (2 dc, ch 1, 2 dc); do not ch or turn; finish off Color B.

Row 3 (right side): With right side facing you, join Color A, with sc in 3rd ch of starting ch at right; *ch 3, work V-st in next sc, ch 3, sc between center 2 dc of next shell; rep from * across, ending last rep with V-st in last sc, ch 3, sc in last dc; do not ch or turn; finish off Color A.

Row 4 (right side): With right side facing you, join Color B with sc in first sc at right; *skip next ch-3 sp, work shell in ch-1 sp of next V-st, skip next ch-3 sp, sc in next sc; rep from * across, ending last rep with work shell in ch-1 sp of last V-st, skip ch-3 sp, sc in last sc. Finish off; weave in all yarn ends.

#15

Stitch multiple: Any even number

Yarn: One color

Instructions

Foundation Row (wrong side): With wrong side facing you, join yarn with sc in first st at right; sc in each rem st; ch 4 (counts as tr on following row), turn.

Row 1 (right side): *Skip next sc, tr in next sc, tr in skipped sc: crossed st made; rep from * across to last sc; tr in last sc; ch 1, turn.

Row 2: Sc in each tr across, ending last rep with sc in 4th ch of turning ch-4; ch 1, turn.

Row 3: Sc in first sc; *ch 3, sc in next sc; rep from * across. Finish off; weave in yarn ends.

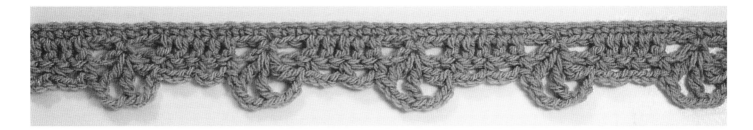

#16

Stitch multiple: 10 + 5 sts

Yarn: One color

Stitch Guide

Shell: In specified st work (tr, ch 3) twice, tr in same st: shell made.

Instructions

Foundation Row (right side): With right side facing you, join yarn with sc in first st at right; sc in each rem st; ch 3 (counts as dc on following row), turn.

Row 1: Dc in next 4 sc; *ch 2, skip next 2 sc, sc in next sc, ch 2, skip next 2 sc, dc in next 5 sc; rep from * across; ch 1, turn.

Row 2: Sc in first dc; *(ch 3, skip next dc, sc in next dc) twice, shell in next sc**; sc in next dc; rep from * across, ending last rep at **; (sc in next dc, ch 3, skip next dc) twice, sc in 3rd ch of turning ch-3. Finish off, weave in yarn ends.

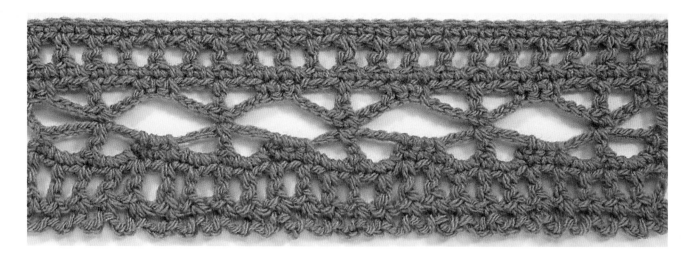

#17

Stitch multiple: 8 + 1 sts

Yarn: One color

Instructions

Foundation Row (right side): With right side facing, join yarn with sc in first st at right; sc in each rem st; ch 4 (counts as a dc and ch-1 sp on following row), turn.

Row 1: Skip next sc, dc in next sc; *ch 1, skip next sc, dc in next sc; rep from * across; ch 1, turn.

Row 2: Sc in each dc and in each ch-1 sp across, ending last rep with sc in turning ch sp, sc in 3rd ch of turning ch, ch 1, turn.

Row 3: Sc in each of first 2 sc; *ch 3, skip 2 sc, dc in next sc, ch 3, skip 2 sc, sc in next 3 sc; rep from * across, ending last rep with sc in last 2 (instead of 3) sc; ch 7 (counts as a tr and ch-3 sp), turn.

Row 4: Sl st in first dc; *ch 7, sl st in next dc; rep from * across, ending last rep with ch 3, tr in last sc; ch 1, turn.

Row 5: Sc in tr; *ch 3, dc in next sl st, ch 3, 3 sc in next ch-7 lp; rep from * across, ending last rep with ch 3, dc in next sl st, ch 3, sc in 4th ch of turning ch-7; ch 1, turn.

Row 6: Sc in first sc; *3 sc in next ch-3 sp, sc in next dc, 3 sc in next ch-3 sp, sc in next 3 sc, 3 sc in next ch-3 sp, sc in next dc; rep from * across, ending last rep with 3 sc in last ch-3 sp, sc in last sc; ch 4 (counts as a dc and ch-1 sp on following row), turn.

Row 7: Skip next sc; dc in next sc; *ch 1, skip next sc, dc in next sc; rep from * across; ch 1, turn.

Row 8: Sc in first dc; *ch 3, sc in next dc; rep from * across ending last rep with sc in 3rd ch of turning ch. Finish off; weave in yarn ends.

#18

Stitch multiple: 8 + 3 sts

Yarn: One color

Stitch Guide:

Shell: Work 7 dc in specified sp: shell made.

Instructions

Foundation Row (right side): With right side facing you, join yarn with sc in first st at right; sc in each rem st; ch 1, turn.

Row 1: Sc in first sc; *ch 3, skip next sc, sc in next sc; rep from * across; ch 1, turn.

Row 2: Sc in first sc, sc in next ch-3 sp; *ch 3, skip next ch-3 sp; shell in next ch-3 sp, ch 3, skip next ch-3 sp, sc in next ch-3 sp; rep from * across, sc in last sc. Finish off; weave in yarn ends.

16

#19

Stitch multiple: 6 + 1 sts

Yarn: Three colors, Color A, Color B and Color C

Stitch Guide

Triple crochet cluster (trCl): *YO hook 2 times; insert hook in specified sp and draw up a lp, (YO and draw through 2 lps on hook) 2 times; rep from * once in same sp, YO and draw through 3 lps on hook: trCl made.

Shell: In same sp work (trCl, ch 6, trCl): shell made.

Instructions

Foundation Row (wrong side): With wrong side facing you, join Color A with sc in first st at right; sc in each rem st; ch 4 (counts as a dc and ch-1 sp on following row), turn.

Row 1 (right side): Skip next sc, dc in next sc; *ch 1, skip next sc, dc in next sc; rep from * across; finish off Color A.

Row 2 (right side): With right side facing, join Color B with sl st in 3rd ch of turning ch at right, ch 3; skip next ch-1 sp, shell in next ch-1 sp; *skip next 2 ch-1 sps, shell in next ch-1 sp; rep from * across, ending last rep with skip last ch-1 sp, dc in last dc. Finish off Color B.

Row 3 (right side): With right side facing, join Color C with sl st in top of ch-3 at right, ch 1; *in next ch-6 lp work (hdc, ch 4) 4 times, hdc in same lp, ch 1; rep from * across, ending sc in last dc. Finish off; weave in yarn ends.

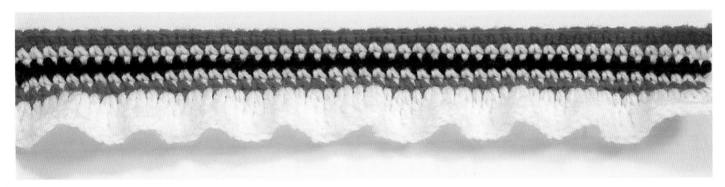

#20

Stitch multiple: Any uneven number

Yarn: Three colors, Color A, Color B, and Color C

Instructions

Note: *All rows are worked with right side facing you.*

Foundation Row (right side): With right side facing you, join Color A with sc in first st at right; sc in each rem st. Finish off Color A.

Row 1 (right side): With right side facing you, join Color B with sc in first sc at right; sc in each rem sc across; finish off Color B.

Row 2 (right side): With right side facing you, join Color C with sl st in first sc at right; ch 2 (counts as a hdc), hdc in each rem sc across; finish off Color C.

Row 3 (right side): With right side facing you, join Color B with sc in top of ch-2 at right; sc in each rem hdc across; finish off Color B.

Row 4 (right side): With right side facing you, join Color A with sc in first sc at right; sc in each rem sc across. Finish off Color A.

Row 5 (right side): With right side facing you, join Color B with sl st in first sc at right; ch 4 (counts as a tr); *work (tr, ch 1, tr) in next sc, tr in next sc; rep from * across. Finish off Color B; weave in yarn ends.

#21

Stitch multiple: 4 + 1 sts

Yarn: Two colors, Color A and Color B

Instructions

Foundation Row (right side): With right side facing, join Color A with sc in first st at right; sc in next st and in each rem st. Finish off Color A.

Row 1 (right side): With right side facing, join Color B with sc in first sc at right, ch 3, work 3 dc in same sc as joining; *skip next 3 sc, in next sc work (sc, ch 3, 3 dc); rep from * across to last 4 sc; skip next 3 sc, sc in last sc. Finish off Color B; weave in all yarn ends.

#22

Stitch multiple: 6 + 1 sts

Yarn: Two colors, Color A and Color B

Stitch Guide

V-Stitch (V-st): In specified st work (dc, ch 3 dc): V-st made.

Shell: In specified sp work 7 dc: shell made.

Instructions

Foundation Row (wrong side): With wrong side facing you, join Color A with sc in first st at right; sc in each rem st; ch 3 (counts as a dc on following row), turn.

Row 1 (right side): *Skip next 2 sc, work V-st in next sc; rep from * across, ending last rep with skip 2 sc, dc in last sc. Finish off Color A.

Row 2 (right side): With right side facing you, join Color B with sc in 3rd ch of turning ch; *work shell in ch-3 sp of next V-st, ** sc in ch-3 sp of next V-st; rep from * across, ending last rep at **; sc in last dc. Finish off Color B.

Row 3 (right side): With right side facing you, join Color A with sc in first sc at right; *ch 4, in center dc of next shell work (dc, ch 2, dc), ch 4, sc in next sc; rep from * across. Finish off Color A; weave in yarn ends.

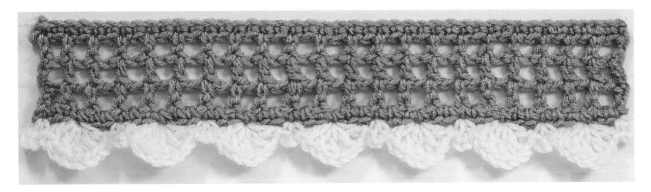

#23

Stitch multiple: 6 + 1 sts

Yarn: Two colors, Color A and Color B

Stitch Guide

Shell: In specified st work [(dc, ch 1) twice, tr, (ch 1, dc) twice]: shell made.

Instructions

Foundation Row (right side): With right side facing you, join Color A with sc in first st at right; sc in each rem st across; ch 4 (counts as a dc and ch-1 sp on following row), turn.

Row 1 (wrong side): Skip next sc, dc in next sc; *ch 1, skip next sc, dc in next sc; rep from * across; ch 4, turn.

Row 2: Dc in next dc; *ch 1, dc in next dc; rep from * across, ending last rep with dc in 3rd ch of turning ch-4; ch 4, turn.

Row 3: Rep Row 2, ending last rep with ch 1, turn.

Row 4: Sc in each dc and in each ch-1 sp across, ending last rep with sc in ch-4 sp, sc in 3rd ch of turning ch-4. Finish off Color A.

Row 5 (right side): With right side facing you, join Color B with sc in first sc at right; ch 3, sc in same sc; *skip 2 sc, work shell in next sc, skip 2 sc, work (sc, ch 3, sc) in next sc; rep from * across. Finish off; weave in yarn ends.

#24

Stitch multiple: Any uneven number

Yarn: One color

Stitch Guide:

Popcorn (PC): Work 5 dc in specified st; drop lp from hook, insert hook from front to back in top of first dc of group, insert hook in dropped lp and draw through: PC made.

Instructions

Foundation Row (right side): With right side facing you, join yarn with sc in first st at right; sc in each rem st across; ch 1, turn.

Row 1: Sc in each sc across, ch 3, turn.

Row 2 (right side): *Work PC in next sc, ch 1, dc in next sc; rep from * across, ch 1, turn.

Row 3: Sc in each dc and in each PC across (**Note:** *Do not work in ch-1 sps)*; ch 1, turn sl st in next sc.

Row 4: Work (sl st, ch 12, sl st) in first sc; *sl st in next sc, work (sl st, ch 12, sl st) in next sc; rep from * across ending with sl st in last sc. Finish off; weave in yarn ends.

#25

Stitch multiple: 4 + 1 sts

Yarn: One color

Stitch Guide

Triple Crochet Cluster (trCl): *YO twice, insert hook in specified st and draw up a lp, (YO and draw through 2 lps on hook) twice; rep from * 2 times more in same st, YO and draw through 4 lps: trCl made.

Shell: In specified sp work (sc, hdc, dc, tr, dc, hdc, sc): shell made.

Instructions

Foundation Row (wrong side): With wrong side facing you, join yarn with sc in first st at right; sc in each rem st; ch 1, turn.

Row 1 (right side): Sc in first sc; *ch 3, skip next sc, trCl in next sc, ch 3, skip next sc, sc in next sc; rep from * across; ch 8 (counts as a dc and ch-5 sp on following row), turn.

Row 2: Dc in next sc; *ch 5, dc in next sc; rep from * across; ch 1, turn.

Row 3: Sc in first dc; *work shell in next ch-5 sp; rep from * across, ending last rep with shell in turning ch sp, sc in 3rd ch of turning ch-8. Finish off; weave in yarn ends.

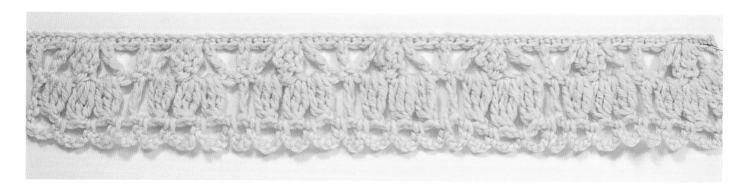

#26

Stitch multiple: 8 + 1 sts

Yarn: One color

Stitch Guide

Triple Crochet Cluster (trCl): *YO twice; insert hook in specified st or sp and draw up a lp, (YO and draw through 2 lps on hook) twice; rep from * 2 times more in same st or sp, YO and draw through all 4 lps on hook: trCl made.

Instructions

Foundation Row (right side): With right side facing you, join yarn with sc in first st at right; sc in each rem st; ch 4 (counts as first tr of following row), turn.

Row 1: Skip next 2 sc, tr in next sc, ch 2, trCl in next sc, ch 2, tr in next sc; *(skip 2 sc, tr in next sc) twice, ch 2, trCl in next sc, ch 2, tr in next sc; rep from * across to last 3 sc, skip 2 sc, tr in last sc; ch 6, turn.

Row 2: *Skip next tr, work trCL in next ch-2 sp, ch 2, trCl in top of next trCl, ch 2, trCl in next ch-2 sp, ch 2, skip next tr, tr in next tr, ch 2; rep from * across, ending last rep with tr in top of turning ch sp; ch 1, turn.

Row 3: Sc in first tr; *ch 5, sc in next ch-2 sp; rep from * across, ending last rep with sc in turning ch sp. Finish off; weave in yarn ends.

#27

Stitch multiple: 12 + 4 sts

Yarn: One color

Stitch Guide:

Double triple crochet (dtr): YO 3 times; insert hook in specified sp and draw up a lp, (YO and draw through 2 lps) 4 times: dtr made.

Shell: In specified lp work (4 tr, 3 dtr, 4 tr): shell made.

Instructions

Foundation Row: (wrong side): With wrong side facing you, join yarn with sc in first st at right; sc in each st across; ch 5 (counts as a dc and ch-2 sp on following row), turn.

Row 1 (right side): Skip next 2 sc, dc in next sc; *ch 2, skip next 2 sc, dc in next sc; rep from * across; ch 5 (counts as a dc and ch-2 sp on following row), turn.

Row 2: Dc in next dc, ch 2, dc in next dc; *ch 8, dc in next dc,** (ch 2, dc in next dc) 3 times; rep from * across, ending last rep at **; ch 2, dc in next dc, ch 2, dc in 3rd ch of turning ch-5; ch 4 (counts as a dc and ch-1 sp on following row), turn.

Row 3: Dc in next dc, ch 1; *dc in next dc, work shell in next ch-8 lp, dc in next dc **, (ch 1, dc in next dc) 2 times, ch 1; rep from * across, ending last rep at **; ch 1, dc in next dc, ch 1, dc in 3rd ch of turning ch. Finish off; weave in yarn ends.

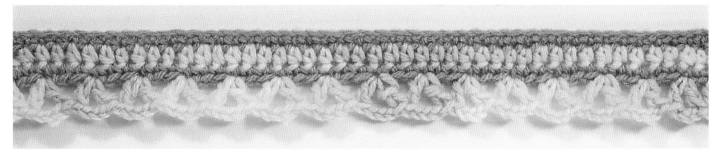

#28

Stitch multiple: 3 + 1 sts

Yarn: Two colors, Color A and Color B

Stitch Guide

V-stitch: (V-st): Work (dc, ch 3, dc) all in same st: V-st made.

Instructions

Note: *All rows are worked with right side facing you.*

Foundation Row (right side): With right side facing you, join Color A with sc in first st at right; sc in each rem st. Finish off Color A.

Row 1 (right side): With right side facing you, join Color B with sl st in first st at right, ch 2 (equals a hdc); hdc in each rem sc across. Finish off Color B.

Row 2 (right side): With right side facing, join Color A with sc in 2nd ch of beg ch-2 at right, sc in each rem hdc across; finish off Color A.

Row 3 (right side): Join Color B with sl st in first sc at right; ch 6 (counts as a dc and ch-3 sp), dc in same st; *skip next 2 sc, work V-st in next sc; rep from * across. Finish off Color B; weave in yarn ends.

#29

Stitch multiple: 4 sts

Yarn: Three colors, Color A, Color B and Color C

Instructions

Foundation Row (wrong side): With wrong side facing you, join Color A with sc in first st at right; sc in each rem st; ch 1, turn.

Row 1 (right side): Sc in each sc across; finish off Color A.

Row 2 (right side): With right side facing you, join Color B with sl st in first sc at right, ch 3 (counts as a dc); *skip next sc, dc in next sc, dc in skipped sc; rep from * across, ending last rep with dc in last sc. Finish off Color B.

Row 3 (right side): With right side facing you, join Color C with sc in 3rd ch of beg ch-3 at right; *ch 4, sc in next dc, ch 6, sc in next dc; rep from * across to last dc, ch 4, sc in last dc. Finish off Color C; weave in yarn ends.

#30

Stitch multiple: 5 + 1 sts

Yarn: One color

Instructions

Foundation Row (right side): With right side facing you, join yarn with sc in first st at right; sc in each rem st; ch 1, turn.

Row 1: Sc in first sc; *ch 5, skip 4 sc, sc in next sc; rep from * across; ch 4 (counts as a tr on following row), turn.

Row 2 (right side): *Work 5 tr in next ch-5 sp, **ch 1; rep from * across, ending last rep at **; tr in last sc; ch 3, turn.

Row 3: *Work (dc, ch 1, dc) in center tr of next 5-tr group, ** ch 3, sc in next ch-1 sp, ch 3; rep from * across, ending last rep at **; ch 3, sc in top of turning ch. Finish off; weave in yarn ends.

#31

Stitch multiple: 12 + 9 sts

Stitch Guide

Shell: In specified lp work (sc, 2 hdc, 9 dc, 2 hdc, sc): shell made.

Double Crochet Cluster (dcCl): *YO, insert hook in specified st and draw up a lp, YO and draw through 2 lps on hook; rep from * 2 times more in same lp, YO and draw through 4 lps: dcCl made.

Instructions

Foundation Row (wrong side): With wrong side facing you, join yarn with sc in first st at right; sc in each rem st; ch 1, turn.

Row 1 (right side): Sc in first sc, ch 3, skip 3 sc, dcCl in next sc, ch 3, skip 3 sc, sc in next sc; *ch 8, sl st in 6th ch from hook: lp formed; ch 1, turn; working from right to left in lp work (sc, 2 hdc, 9 dc, 2 hdc, sc), ch 2, skip 3 sc, sc in next sc; ch 3, skip 3 sc, dcCl in next sc, ch 3, skip 3 sc, sc in next sc; rep from * across; ch 8 (counts as a tr and ch-4 sp on following row), turn.

Row 2: *Sl st in top of next dcCl, ch 4; **(sc in next dc of shell, ch 4, skip next dc of shell) 4 times, sc in last dc of shell; ch 4; rep from * across, ending last rep at **; tr in last sc. Finish off; weave in yarn ends.

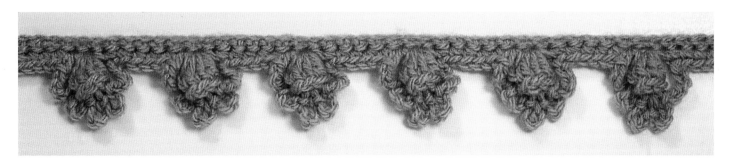

#32

Stitch multiple: 7 + 4 sts

Yarn: One color

Stitch Guide

Popcorn (PC): Work 5 dc in specified st; drop lp from hook, insert hook from front to back in top of first dc of group, insert hook in dropped lp and draw through lp on hook: PC made.

Instructions

Foundation Row (wrong side): With wrong side facing you, join yarn with sc in first st at right; sc in each rem st across; ch 1, turn.

Row 1: Sc in first 5 sc; *ch 5, work PC in next sc; (ch 5, sl st through center opening of PC just made) 3 times; ch 5**; sc in next 6 sc; rep from * across, ending last rep at **; sc in last 5 sc. Finish off; weave in yarn ends.

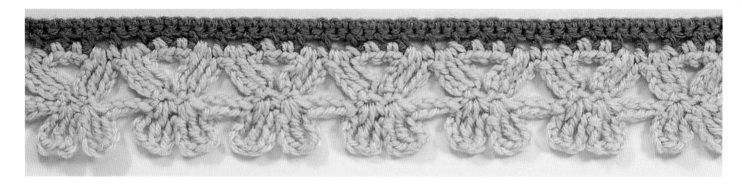

#33

Stitch multiple: 8 + 1 sts

Yarn: Two Colors, Color A and Color B

Stitch Guide

Petal: Work (sc, ch 4, tr, ch 4, sc) all in same st or sp: Petal made.

Instructions

Foundation Row (wrong side): With wrong side facing you, join Color A with sc in first st at right, sc in each rem st; ch 3 (counts as hdc and ch-1 sp on following row), turn.

Row 1 (right side): Skip next sc, hdc in next sc; *ch 1, skip next sc, hdc in next sc; rep from * across. Finish off Color A.

Row 2 (right side): With right side facing you, join Color B with sc in 2nd ch of turning ch-3; *work Petal in next ch-1 sp; (ch 1, skip next hdc, sc in next ch-1 sp) twice; ch 1, skip next hdc, work Petal in next ch-1 sp**; ch 1, skip next hdc; rep from * across, ending last rep at **; sc in last hdc; ch 7 (counts as tr and ch-3 sp on following row), turn.

Row 3: *Sc in tr of each of next 2 Petals**; ch 5; rep from * across, ending last rep at **; ch 3, tr in last sc; ch 1, turn.

Row 4: Sc in tr, ch 2; *work Petal in each of next 2 sc**; ch 4; rep from * across, ending last rep at **; ch 2, sc in 4th ch of turning ch-7. Finish off Color B; weave in yarn ends.

#34

Stitch multiple: 3 + 1 sts

Yarn: One Color

Stitch Guide

V-stitch (V-st): In specified st work (dc, ch 2, dc): V-st made.

Instructions

Foundation Row (right side): With right side facing you, join yarn with sc in first st at right; sc in each rem st across; ch 1, turn.

Row 1: Sc in first sc, ch 5 (counts as a dc and ch-2 sp), dc in same sc; *skip 2 sc, work V-st in next sc; rep from * across; ch 6 (counts as a dc and ch-3 sp on following row), turn.

Row 2: Skip next ch-2 sp and skip next dc; dc in next dc; working in front of dc just made, dc in skipped dc: cross stitch made; *ch 3, skip next ch-2 sp and next dc, dc in next dc; working in front of dc just made, dc in skipped dc; rep from * across, ending last rep with ch 3, dc in 3rd ch of turning ch-6; ch 5, turn.

Row 3: *Skip ch-3 sp, sl st in next dc, ch 3, sl st in next dc, ch 5; rep from * across, ending last rep with ch 5, sc in 3rd ch of turning ch-6. Finish off; weave in yarn ends.

#35

Stitch multiple: 6 + 1 sts

Yarn: Two colors, Color A and Color B

Instructions

Foundation Row (right side): With right side facing you, join Color A with sc in first st at right; sc in each st across. Finish off Color A.

Row 1 (right side): With right side facing you, join Color B with sc in first sc at right; *skip 2 sc, in next sc work (dc, ch 5, dc), skip 2 sc, sc in next sc; rep from * across; ch 5, turn.

Row 2: Dc in base of ch; *sc in 3rd ch of next ch-5 sp, (dc, ch 5, dc) in next sc; rep from * across, ending last rep with sc in 3rd ch of last ch-5 sp, work (dc, ch 2, dc) in last sc. Finish off Color B.

Row 3 (right side): With right side facing you, join Color A with sc in first dc at right; *work 7 tr in next sc, sl st in 3rd ch of next ch-5 sp; rep from * across, ending last rep with sc in 3rd ch of turning ch-5. Finish off Color A.

Row 4 (right side): With right side facing you, join Color B with sc in first sc at right; *(sl st in next tr, ch 4) 6 times, sl st in next tr: 6 ch-4 lps made; skip next sc; rep from * across, ending by working sc in last sc. Finish off Color B; weave in yarn ends.

#36

Stitch multiple: 5 + 1 sts

Yarn: Two colors, Color A and Color B

Stitch Guide

Triple Crochet Cluster (trCl): *YO twice; insert hook in specified sp, YO and draw up a lp; (YO and draw through 2 lps on hook) twice: 2 lps rem on hook; rep from * 2 times more: 4 lps rem on hook; YO and draw through all 4 lps on hook: trCl made.

Shell: In specified sp work (sc, ch 1, hdc, ch 1, dc, ch 1, tr, ch 1, dc, ch 1, hdc, ch 1, sc): shell made.

Instructions

Foundation Row (right side): With right side facing you, join Color A with sc in first st at right; sc in each rem st; ch 1, turn.

Row 1: Sc in first sc; *ch 4, skip next 4 sc, sc in next sc; rep from * across; ch 6 (counts as a tr and ch-2 sp on following row), turn.

Row 2: *Work trCl in next ch-4 sp, ch 4; rep from * across, ending last rep with ch 2 (instead of ch 4), tr in last sc. Finish off Color A.

Row 3 (right side): With right side facing, join Color B with sl st in 4th ch of beg ch-6, ch 2, sc in top of next trCl; *shell in next ch-4 sp; rep from * across, ending last rep with sc in top of last trCl, ch 2, sl st in top of last tr. Finish off; weave in yarn ends.

#37

Stitch multiple: 8 + 3 sts

Yarn: Two colors, Color A and Color B

Instructions

Foundation Row (right side): With right side facing you, join Color A with sc in first st at right; sc in next st and each rem st across. Finish off Color A.

Row 1 (right side): With right side facing you, join Color B with sl st in back lp only of first sc at right, sl st in back lp only of next 2 sc; *skip next 2 sc, in both lps of next sc work [(dc, ch 4) 5 times, dc]; skip next 2 sc, sl st in back lp only of next 3 sc; rep from * across. Finish off Color B; weave in all yarn ends.

#38

Stitch multiple: 8 + 4 sts

Yarn: One color

Stitch Guide

Triple Crochet Cluster (trCl): *YO twice, insert hook in specified sp and draw up a lp, (YO and draw through 2 lps on hook) twice; rep from * 2 times in same sp, YO and draw through 4 lps on hook: trCl made.

Instructions

Foundation Row (right side): With right side facing you, join yarn with sc in first st at right; sc in each rem st; ch 3 (counts as a dc on following row), turn.

Row 1: Dc in next sc and in each rem sc across; ch 3, turn.

Row 2: Dc in next 3 dc; *ch 4, skip 4 dc, dc in next 4 dc; rep from * across, ending last rep with dc in top of turning ch; ch 1, turn.

Row 3: Sc in first 4 dc, *ch 5, trCl in next ch-4 sp, ch 5, sc in next 4 dc; rep from * across, ending last rep with sc in top of turning ch; ch 1, turn.

Row 4: *Sc in next 4 sc, 5 sc in ch-5 sp, work (sl st, ch 6, sl st) in top of trCl, 5 sc in next ch-5 sp, rep from * across, ending last rep with sc in last 4 sc. Finish off; weave in yarn ends.

#39

Stitch multiple: 8 + 1 sts

Yarn: One color

Stitch Guide

Shell: In specified st work (tr, ch 1) twice, tr in same st: shell made.

Instructions

Foundation Row (wrong side): With wrong side facing you, join yarn with sc in first st at right; sc in each rem st; ch 1, turn.

Row 1 (right side): Sc in each of first 3 sc; *ch 1, skip next sc, shell in next sc, ch 1, skip next sc, sc in next 5 sc; rep from * across, ending last rep with sc in last 3 (instead of 5) sc; ch 1, turn.

Row 2: Sc in each of first 3 sc; *ch 4, in center tr of next shell work (dc, ch 3, dc), ch 4, sc in each of next 5 sc; rep from * across, ending last rep with sc in last 3 (instead of 5) sc. Finish off; weave in yarn ends.

#40

Stitch multiple: 12 + 1 sts

Yarn: Two colors, Color A and Color B

Stitch Guide

Picot: Ch 3, sl st in 3rd ch from hook: picot made.

Instructions

Foundation Row (right side): With right side facing you, join Color A with sc in first st at right; sc in each rem st across; ch 1, turn.

Row 1: Sc in first sc; *ch 5, skip next 3 sc, sc in next sc; rep from * across; ch 5 (counts as a dc and ch-2 sp on following row), turn.

Row 2: *Sc in next ch-5 sp, work 8 dc in next ch-5 sp, sc in next ch-5 sp**; ch 4; rep from * across, ending last rep at **; ch 2, dc in last sc. Finish off Color A.

Row 3: With right side facing you, join Color B with sc in 3rd ch of turning ch-5 at right, ch 1; *(dc in back lp only, work picot) in each of next 7 dc, dc in back lp only of next dc, ch 1**; sc in next ch-4 sp, ch 1; rep from * across, ending last rep at **; sc in last dc. Finish off; weave in yarn ends.

#41

Stitch multiple: 7 sts

Yarn: One color

Stitch Guide

Double triple crochet (dtr): YO 3 times, insert hook in specified st and draw up a lp, (YO and draw through 2 lps) 4 times: dtr made.

Shell: In specified st work (2 tr, dtr, 2 tr): shell made.

Instructions

Foundation Row (wrong side): With wrong side facing you, join yarn with sc in first st at right, sc in each rem st; ch 1, turn.

Row 1 (right side): Sc in first sc; * ch 4, skip 2 sc, shell in next sc; ch 9, turn; working from right to left, join ch-9 lp with sl st in first tr of shell, ch 1, turn; working now from right to left, work 11 sc in ch-9 lp, ch 4, skip 2 sc, sc in next 2 sc; rep from * across, ending last rep with sc in last sc. Finish off; weave in yarn ends.

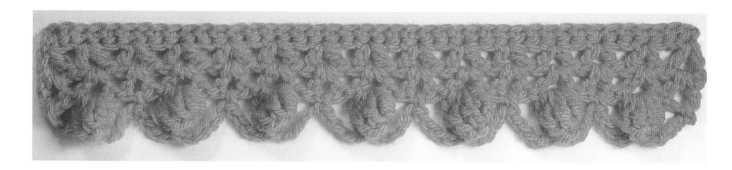

#42

Stitch multiple: 6 + 1 sts

Yarn: One color

Stitch Guide

V-stitch (V-st): In specified st work (dc, ch 1, dc): V-st made.

Note: *When working into V-st on following rows, work into the ch-1 sp.*

Popcorn (PC): Work 5 tr in specified sp; drop lp from hook, insert hook from front to back in top of first tr of group; insert hook in dropped lp and draw through lp on hook: PC made.

Instructions

Foundation Row (wrong side): With wrong side facing you, join yarn with sc in first st at right; sc in each rem st, ch 4 (counts as dc and ch-1 sp on following row), turn.

Row1 (right side): Dc in first sc; *skip next 2 sc, V-st in next sc; rep from * across; ch 1, turn.

Row 2: Sl st in first dc and in ch-1 sp of next V-st; ch 4 (counts as dc and ch-1 sp), dc in same ch-1 sp, V-st in next V-st and in each V-st across, ending with V-st in turning ch-4 sp; ch 1, turn.

Row 3: Sc in first dc, sc in ch-1 sp of next V-st; *ch 5, PC in next V-st, ch 5**; sc in next V-st; rep from * across, ending last rep at **; sc in ch-4 sp, sc in 3rd ch of same ch-4 sp. Finish off; weave in yarn ends.

#43

Stitch multiple: 10 + 1 sts

Yarn: Two colors, Color A and Color B

Stitch Guide

Shell: In specified st work (3 dc, ch 3, 3 dc): shell made.

Instructions

Foundation Row (right side): With right side facing you, join Color A with sc in first st at right; sc in next st and in each st across, changing to Color B in last st; with Color B, ch 1, turn. Finish off Color A.

Row 1: With Color B, sc in first 3 sc; *skip next 2 sc, shell in next sc, skip next 2 sc**; sc in next 5 sc; rep from * across, ending last rep at **; sc in last 3 sc; ch 1, turn.

Row 2 (right side): Sc in first 3 sc; *ch 2, work 7 dc in ch-3 sp of next shell, ch 2**; sc in next 5 sc; rep from * across, ending last rep at **; sc in last 3 sc. Finish off Color B.

Row 3 (right side): With right side facing you, join Color A with sc in first sc at right; sc in next 2 sc; *2 sc in next ch-2 sp, sc in next 3 dc, work (sc, ch 3, sc) in next dc, sc in next 3 dc; 2 sc in next ch-2 sp**; skip next 2 sc, work 5 dc in next sc, skip next 2 sc; rep from * across, ending last rep at **; sc in last 3 sc. Finish off Color A; weave in all yarn ends.

#44

Stitch multiple: 10 + 5 sts

Yarn: One color

Instructions

Foundation Row (right side): With right side facing you, join yarn with sc in first st at right; sc in each rem st, ch 3 (counts as dc on following row), turn.

Row 1: Dc in next 4 sc; *ch 5, skip next 5 sc, dc in next 5 sc; rep from * across; ch 1, turn.

Row 2: Sc in each of next 5 dc; *ch 5, sc in next 5 dc; rep from * across, working last sc in 3rd ch of ch-3; ch 1, turn.

Row 3: Sc in first 5 sc; *ch 2; working in front of ch-5 lps on Rows 1 and 2, tr in center sc of 5-sc group skipped on Row 1, ch 2, sc in next 5 sc; rep from * across; ch 1, turn.

Row 4: Sc in first 5 sc; *2 hdc in next ch-2 sp, in next tr work (dc, ch 2, dc), 2 hdc in next ch-2 sp, sc in next 5 sc; rep from * across. Finish off; weave in yarn ends.

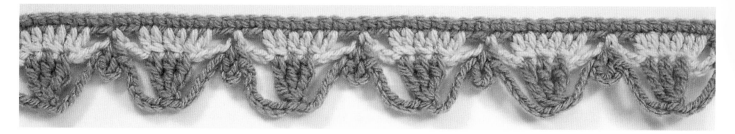

#45

Stitch multiple: 9 + 1

Yarn: Two colors, Color A and Color B

Stitch Guide

Double Crochet Cluster (dcCl): YO, insert hook in specified st and draw up a lp, YO and draw through 2 lps: 2 lps rem on hook; YO, insert hook in next st and draw up a lp, YO and draw through 2 lps: 3 lps rem on hook; YO and draw through 3 lps on hook: dcCl made.

Triple Crochet Cluster (trCl): *YO twice, insert hook in top of next dcCl and draw up a lp, (YO and draw through 2 lps) twice; rep from * 2 times more, YO and draw through 4 lps on hook: trCl made.

Instructions

Note: *All rows are worked with right side facing you.*

Foundation Row (right side): With right side facing you, join Color A with sc in first st at right; sc in each rem st. Finish off Color A.

Row 1 (right side): With right side facing you, join Color B with sc in first sc at right; *ch 3, skip next sc, (dcCl over next 2 sc) 3 times, ch 3, skip next sc, sc in next sc; rep from * across. Finish off Color B.

Row 2 (right side): With right side facing you, join Color A with sc in first sc at right; *ch 7, work trCl over next 3 dcCls, ch 7,** work (sc, ch 4, sc) in next sc; rep from * across, ending last rep at **; sc in last sc. Finish off; weave in yarn ends.

#46

Stitch multiple: 9 + 7 sts

Yarn: Two colors, Color A and Color B

Stitch Guide

V-stitch (V-st): In specified st work (dc, ch 1, dc): V-st made.

Fan: In specified sp work 9 tr: fan made.

Popcorn (PC): Work 4 dc in specified sp; drop lp from hook, insert hook from front to back through top of first dc of group, insert hook in dropped lp and draw through lp on hook: PC made.

Instructions

Foundation Row (right side): With right side facing you, join Color A with sc in first st at right; sc in each rem st; ch 4 (counts as dc and ch-1 sp on following row), turn.

Row 1: Dc in first sc; *skip next 2 sc, work V-st in next sc; rep from * across; ch 1, turn.

Row 2 (right side): Sc in first dc, sc in next ch-1 sp; *in ch-1 sp of next V-st work (2 dc, ch 2, 2 dc)**; sc in next ch-1 sp, ch 3, sc in next ch-1 sp; rep from * across, ending last rep at **; sc in turning ch-4 sp, sc in 3rd ch of turning ch-4. Finish off Color A.

Row 3 (right side): With right side facing you, join Color B with sc in first sc at right; *ch 3, in next ch-2 sp work (PC, ch 4, PC), ch 3**; sc in next ch-3 sp; rep from * across, ending last rep at **; skip next 3 sc, sc in last sc. Finish off Color B.

Row 4 (right side): With right side facing you, join Color A with sl st in first sc at right, ch 4 (counts as a tr); *work fan in next ch-4 sp**; ch 3, sc in next sc, ch 3; rep from * across, ending last rep at **; tr in last sc. Finish off Color A.

Row 5 (right side): With right side facing you, join Color B with sc in first tr of first fan at right; (ch 3, sc in next tr) 8 times; *ch 3, sc in next sc, (ch 3, sc in next tr) 9 times; rep from * across. Finish off Color B; weave in all yarn ends.

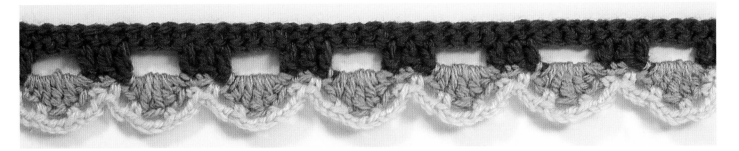

#47

Stitch multiple: 6 + 3 sts

Yarn: Three colors, Color A, Color B and Color C

Stitch Guide:

Shell: In specified sp work (sc, hdc, dc, tr, dc, hdc, sc): shell made.

Instructions

Foundation Row (wrong side): With wrong side facing you, join Color A with sc in first st at right; sc in each rem st; ch 3 (counts as a dc on following row), turn.

Row 1 (right side): Dc in each of next 2 sc; *ch 3, skip 3 sc, dc in next 3 sc; rep from * across. Finish off Color A.

Row 2 (right side): With right side facing you, skip ch-3 at right, join Color B with sc in next dc; *work shell in next ch-3 sp, sc in center dc of next 3-dc group; rep from * across. Finish off Color B.

Row 3 (right side): With right side facing you, join Color C in first sc at right; *sc in first sc of next shell, ch 3, skip hdc, sc in dc, ch 3, skip tr, sc in dc, ch 3, skip hdc, sc in sc; rep from * across, ending last rep with sc in last sc. Finish off; weave in yarn ends.

#48

Stitch Multiple: 8 + 4 sts

Yarn: Three colors, Color A, Color B and Color C

Stitch Guide

Leaf: Ch 7, sc in 2nd ch from hook, hdc in next ch, 2 dc in next ch, hdc in next ch, sc in next ch, sl st in last ch: leaf made.

Stem: Ch 10, skip first 5 chs, sl st in next 5 chs: stem made.

Popcorn (PC): Work 5 tr in specified sp; drop lp from hook, insert hook from front to back in top of first tr of group, insert hook in dropped lp and draw through lp on hook: PC made.

Instructions

Note: *When working sl sts, to keep them from being too tight, be sure to bring lps up onto working area of hook.*

Foundation Row (wrong side): With wrong side facing you, join Color A with sc in first st at right; sc in each rem st across; turn.

Row 1 (right side): Sl st in first 5 sc; *work leaf, sl st in next sc, work stem, sl st in next sc, work leaf**; sl st in next 6 sc; rep from * across, ending last rep at **; sl st in last 5 sc. Finish off Color A.

Row 2 (right side): With right side facing you, join Color B with sl st in tip of first leaf at right; *ch 3, in ch-5 sp at top of next stem work (PC, ch 4) 3 times, PC in same ch-5 sp; ch 3**; insert hook in tips of each of next 2 leaves, YO and draw through all 3 lps on hook: leaves joined; rep from * across, ending last rep at **; sl st in tip of last leaf. Finish off Color B.

Row 3 (right side): With right side facing you, join Color C with sc in first sl st on first leaf at right; *[in next ch-4 sp work (dc, ch 3) twice, dc in same sp] 3 times, sc in next sc; rep from * across, ending last rep with sc in last sl st. Finish off; weave in yarn ends.

#49

Stitch multiple: 3 + 2 sts

Yarn: Four colors, Color A, Color B, Color C and Color D

Instructions

Foundation Row (right side): With right side facing you, join Color A with sc in first st at right; sc in each st; ch 1, turn.

Row 1: Sc in each sc across. Finish off Color A.

Row 2 (right side): With right side facing, join Color B with sl st in first sc at right; ch 4 (counts as a dc and ch-1 sp), skip next sc, work (dc, ch 2, dc) in next sc; *skip next 2 sc, in next sc work (dc, ch 2, dc); rep from * across to last 2 sc, ch 1, skip next sc, dc in last sc; ch 1, turn.

Row 3: Sc in first dc, sc in ch-1 sp; *sc in next dc, 2 sc in ch-2 sp, sc in next dc; rep from * across. ending last rep with sc in ch 4 sp, sc in 3rd ch of ch-4 sp. Finish off Color B.

Row 4 (right side): With right side facing you, join Color A with sc in first sc at right, sc in next sc and in each sc across; ch 1, turn.

Row 5: Sc in first sc and in each sc across. Finish off Color A.

Row 6 (right side): With right side facing you, join Color C with sl st in first sc at right, ch 3 (equals a dc), dc in each sc to last sc, 2 sc in last sc. Finish off Color C.

Row 7: (right side): With right side facing, join Color D with sl st in top of beg ch-3 at right, ch 6 (counts as a dc and ch-3 sp), dc in base of ch; *skip next dc, in next dc work (dc, ch 3, dc); rep from * across. Finish off; weave in yarn ends.

#50

Stitch multiple: 6 + 1 sts

Yarn: One color

Stitch Guide

Popcorn (PC): Work 4 tr in specified st; drop lp from hook, insert hook from front to back in top of first tr of group, insert hook in dropped lp and draw through lp on hook: PC made.

Instructions

Foundation Row: With wrong side facing you, join yarn with sc in first st at right; sc in each rem st, ch 4 (counts as tr on following row), turn.

Row 1 (right side): (Ch 4, sl st in 4th ch from hook) 3 times, tr in base of turning ch; *ch 1, skip next 2 sc, work PC in next sc, ch 1; skip next 2 sc, in next sc work [tr, (ch 4, sl st in 4th ch from hook) 3 times, tr]; rep from * across. Finish off; weave in yarn ends.